Idleness Is
the Root of
All Love

Idleness Is
the Root of
All Love

Christa Reinig
translated by Ilze Mueller

CALYX Books
Corvallis, Oregon

The publication of this book was supported with grants from the National Endowment for the Arts, the Oregon Arts Commission, the Oregon Institute of Literary Arts, and the William A. Gillmore Fund of the Oregon Community Foundation.

Originally published in 1984 as
Müssiggang ist aller liebe anfang
© Verlag Eremiten-Presse, Düsseldorf, 1984

English translation © 1991 by Ilze Mueller

Cover art, *Fringed Gentian*, oil, by Kristina Kennedy Daniels
Cover and book design
by Darryla Green-McGrath and Cheryl McLean

CALYX BOOKS are distributed to the trade through major library distributors, jobbers, and most small press distributors, including: Airlift, Bookpeople, Bookslinger, Inland Book Co., Pacific Pipeline, and Small Press Distribution. For personal orders or other information write: CALYX BOOKS, PO Box B, Corvallis, OR 97339, 503-753-9384.

∞

The paper in this book meets the guidelines for permanence and durability of the Committee on Production Guidelines for Book Longevity of the Council on Library Resources and the minimum requirements of the American National Standard for the Permanence of Paper for Printed Library Materials Z38.48-1984.

Library of Congress Cataloging-in-Publication Data
Reinig, Christa.
    [Müssiggang ist aller Liebe Anfang. English]
    Idleness is the root of all love : poems / by Christa Reinig; translated by Ilze Mueller.
        p. cm.
    Translation of: Müssiggang ist aller Liebe Anfang.
    ISBN 0-934971-22-6 (alk.paper): $18.95. — ISBN 0-934971-21-8 (pbk.): $10.00.
    I. Title
PT2678.E347M813 1991   831'.914—dc2091-11708
                                                    CIP

Printed in the U.S.A.

ACKNOWLEDGMENTS

I should like to thank Ruth-Ellen Boetcher Joeres, Toni McNaron, and Janet Wheelock, who generously gave their time in reading the manuscript of my translation, contributed many helpful suggestions, and encouraged me as the work progressed.

Ilze Mueller
Translator

CONTENTS

INTRODUCTION

"I am a member of the lesbian nation, even if I didn't want to be, I would have to be."[1] This is how Christa Reinig positions herself—as a woman, a writer, and an activist—in an essay she wrote the same year that *Idleness Is the Root of All Love* was published. Virtually everything she has written (certainly everything she has written since her 1976 novel *Entmannung* [Demanning]) can be read as an elaboration of this statement. It can also be read as an answer to the implicit question: why? Why does she "have to be," regardless of whether or not she might "want to be"?

In an essay entitled "Morality and Taste," Reinig provides one unequivocal answer: "90% of all living creatures lying around on our streets, abused and slaughtered, are not rats, cats, dogs, pigs, but women."[2] And it is up to us—to women—to put an end to this woman-hating violence. Feminism, for Reinig, is not about equality (equal rights or equal opportunity). Nor is it about identity (the search for or construction of a female "I"). Rather, it is about women's right to be who they please and live as they choose without being attacked, interfered with, or subjugated by men. Feminism, then, is the struggle to create such a space: on our streets, in our relationships, in our literatures, and in our heads.

Reinig writes for women and against femininity. Her approach is blunt and unapologetic. She sharpens the focus on unpleasant truths until they become hyperreal: reality heightened to satire. In the glare of her gaze, all humor eventually turns black. As she sees it, there is a war going on and women's lives are at stake. There is no time for feminine niceties. In such times, she insists, feminism must be uncompromising and tough, not gentle or sentimental. As she once put it, "We—feminists—are not the Salvation Army. We can't spend our time comforting and commiserating with women who have been victimized. What we must fight is women's victimization."[3] Thus, Reinig has always qualified the West German feminist motto that "women together are strong" with the reminder that we can only be strong together if we are also strong in ourselves.

As she points out, the times we live in give us no choice. If we want something, we must be able and willing to pay. Certainly, she herself has done so. As a young writer in East Germany in the 1950s, she refused to "correct" her work in line with the official "socialist realist" doctrines; her refusal cost her the right to be published in the country in which she lived and, eventually, her ability to live there. In West Germany, where she has lived since 1964, she has been honored with some of the most prestigious literary prizes, but not with the public recognition generally accorded a major writer. Once again, it is a price she has paid for the right to go her own way. Around 1980, for example, she decided to move from the prestigious and mainstream presses with whom she had worked exclusively thus far to work more with an alternative feminist press: the Munich-based Frauenoffensive.[4] And so, just as in her twenties she refused to conform to the literary codes of a socialist state-imposed dogma, she now, in her fifties and sixties, refuses to cater to the codes of the West German literary establishment and capitalist cultural marketplace.

This nonconformity is evidenced in her writing itself. In a time when the multi-layered complexity of modernist and postmodern styles continues to be prized in cultural establishment circles, Reinig has been moving in precisely the opposite direction, writing more and more simply. Her texts have the simplicity of a weapon directed straight at its target, a tool honed to precision, a language in which all ballast has been cast off. It is the simplicity of a stance pared down to nonnegotiable beliefs, convictions, truths, and necessities. It is simple, because, in the most literal sense, it is radical.

Rather than argue against something she is against, she simply sets it right. Refusing to be bound by structures and values that she—a woman, a lesbian, an aging person, a physically impaired person—cannot accept because they judge her unacceptable, she imaginatively sets herself outside their purview. In the process, as she writes about "outsiders," but *from the inside*, the alternative space she imagines begins to materialize. She writes it into being.

Reinig's radical gesture of inverting the traditional categories "margin" and "center" creates the space in which the story of *Idleness Is the Root of all Love* can be told. It is the story of a year in the life of two women: companion lovers[5] in a contemporary West German metropolis. In the pattern of women's traditional record-keeping and meditation on the everyday—a tradition that includes diaries, calendars, albums, and books of hours—the poet records the daily events in their life together. What the poems (one poem for each day of the year) describe is the extraordinary ordinariness of women's shared lives: ordinary because that is what the quotidian, for the most part, is; extraordinary because it exists in a space that must first be cleared, a space that is "a world of women only."[6] In that sense, the space created by this calendar of poems has a utopian dimension. For, as Adrienne Rich writes in "Transcendental Etude":

...*two women, eye to eye*
measuring each other's spirit, each other's
limited desire,

> *a whole new poetry beginning here.*[7]

Angelika Bammer
German Department
Emory University
March 26, 1991

ENDNOTES

[1]Christa Reinig, "Der Wolf und die Frau ['The Wolf and the Woman']," in
    Der Wolf und die Witwen [The Wolf and the Widows] (Munich:
    Frauenoffensive, 1981):13.
[2]Christa Reinig, "Moral und Geschmack [Morality and Taste]," *Die schwarze
    Botin* [The Black Messenger] 4 (June 1977):3-4.
[3]From a discussion I had with Christa Reinig in Munich in 1980 about the
    state of West German feminism.
[4]Reinig's main publisher has been the small, but exclusive, Eremiten press,
    with whom she works to this day. She has also published with two of West
    Germany's largest and internationally known commercial presses,
    Luchterhand and dtv [Deutscher Taschenbuch Verlag]. From the early eighties
    on, however, she has increasingly been publishing new works (and reprinting
    old ones) with Frauenoffensive.
[5]I take the term from Monique Wittig and Sande Zeig, *Lesbian Peoples: The
    Material for a Dictionary* (New York: Avon, 1979).
[6]I take the term from Adrienne Rich's poem, "Natural Resources," in *The Dream
    of a Common Language: Poems 1974-1977* (New York: W.W. Norton, 1978):
    61.
[7]Adrienne Rich, "Transcendental Etude," in *The Dream of a Common Language*:
    76.

For Pauli
through Pauli
with Pauli

January

1 *SUNDAY*

Of this world not even
the dust belongs to us
when we are dead, we'll be buried
in the earth of our enemies

2 *MONDAY*

Sleeping giant woman
she dreams
a country
without men

3 *TUESDAY*

My fingertips grasp:
I am loved
if you cease to be, I cease to be
you make me mortal

4 *WEDNESDAY*

What are you thinking?—You!
Are you sad?—I am happy
when I was still unable to love
I laughed a lot

5 *THURSDAY*

Again she hasn't come
I close the window
there is nothing that's faithful
except pictures

6 *FRIDAY*   I love you
                      my problem
                      you love me
                      your problem

7 *SATURDAY*   I imagine her calling me up
                      saying: *It's over!* Then I feel
                      the pain drawing near
                      life's been treating me too well I think

8 *SUNDAY*   Let's die together—we both shed tears
                      at this decision
                      as if that's not enough we quickly read
                                Tristan and Isolde
                      insanely funny

9 *MONDAY*   Another body
                      dying next to me
                      what do I know about it

10 *TUESDAY*   *Don't leave me, swear to me you won't!*
                      I swear: If I ever
                      have to separate from you
                      I'll take you with me

11 WEDNESDAY   My woman is ill, I say
                       Goodnessme! says the neighbor lady
                       (and thinks cleaning woman)

12 THURSDAY   There's no way you can die
                       impossible
                       to resign myself to that
                       so I'll force it

13 FRIDAY   Rat-a-tat on the windowframe
                       jerks me awake
                       pattering rain
                       I dreamed you were crying

14 SATURDAY   On how many burning roads
                       I've conquered the force of gravity
                       simply: one foot in front of the other
                       if only you knew

15 SUNDAY   You sit with your back to the light
                       the sky shines through you
                       out of your eyes
                       it beams upon me

16 *MONDAY*   My thirsty fingers
                bathe in your hair
                part it superfluously
                as though there were lice there

17 *TUESDAY*   Out of my desert
                I hurled myself into you
                your arm is the last barrier
                don't leave me

18 *WEDNESDAY* Having a lonely breakfast
                I swallow and feel
                the scar of your operation
                on my belly

19 *THURSDAY*   If I were a persian cat
                with a diesel engine
                you would have fulfilled
                all three wishes at once

20 *FRIDAY*   She's got a pimple on her belly
                perhaps it's a cancerous growth
                we avoid each other's eyes
                talk of something else

21 SATURDAY   Psychophysiopatho-
                   logologologology
                   time doesn't pass
                   when you're not here

22 SUNDAY   The suture is out—for weeks
                   it festered through the skin of the belly
                   I'd love to hang
                   the surgeon by it

23 MONDAY   You drove past me
                   and didn't see me
                   were you talking
                   with me in thought?

24 TUESDAY   A shrewd S.O.B.
                   sicked us on each other
                   even before we locked eyes:
                   the sparks are still flying

25 WEDNESDAY   In deep sleep
                   they open and close
                   a woman's hands
                   they go on working

26 *THURSDAY*   In my happiness
one pain
it won't last
and that's all right

27 *FRIDAY*   Special identifying marks:
dreams about cats

28 *SATURDAY*   You don't call
I am sick with worry
the reason we live apart
is so as not to get frazzled

29 *SUNDAY*   You've gone
your body
keeps breathing
in this room

30 *MONDAY*   Come to realize again
that the hurts
of our childhood
are incurable

31 *TUESDAY*   Change that adds up wrong
makes little holes
in great love

February

1 *WEDNESDAY*   Behind my glasses there sits a man
                     he looks out the window
                     he sees that I'm a woman
                     I can't change that

2 *THURSDAY*   *The woman behind the great man*
                     is my comrade in arms
                     I who am no man's woman
                     can hardly wait

3 *FRIDAY*   I tolerate your preference
                     ma'am—but the fact that you
                     feel attracted to men
                     is nobody's business but your own

4 *SATURDAY*   So what are we waiting for?
                     for the gods—I beg your pardon!
                     for the goddesses of course

5 *SUNDAY*   The equality of man and woman
                     is clear and evident:
                     Woe to the vanquished

6 *MONDAY*

Pinching men's asses
wanting to rape them
paying for their coffee
that's not it

7 *TUESDAY*

Female masochism
is scientifically proven:
a jew who enjoyed Auschwitz
that's what I'm supposed to be

8 *WEDNESDAY*

They feed him and nurse him
and keep him clean
reproduce his kind
worms that don't turn

9 *THURSDAY*

Course for women
using public transportation
—first lesson—
How do I take up more room

10 *FRIDAY*

Lesbians are no longer the tail
prostitutes lie behind us
we've caught up with pickpockets—
soon
we'll be as popular as migrant workers

11 SATURDAY   Being german and being a woman
                   you stand on two skis
                   which take off under you
                   in two directions

12 SUNDAY   Throw
                   your eight-year-old son
                   from the balcony
                   and you're saved

13 MONDAY   The women's movement
                   as a labor union for mothers
                   is a labor union for sons
                   we, however, are daughters

14 TUESDAY   I'll either manage
                   to tune out
                   the bellowing men
                   or I'll croak

15 WEDNESDAY   If the gorilla should
                   perish as well
                   I'd be
                   terribly sorry

16 THURSDAY When stupidity and marriage
no longer hurt or cost you
a box on the ear, only your money
you can be cured, maybe

17 FRIDAY Woman is not a primate
she comes from the ocean
Sappho is older
than Oedipus the ape-father

18 SATURDAY Whole women do not submit
broken women are thrown away
what's left is the one that's half-broken
the manswoman

19 SUNDAY When the word *fascism* is mentioned
maybe there is a workshop
to cure it
discussion, though, won't do

20 MONDAY A chinese man has raped
a black woman—I break off
conversation with a male german
friend
red thread of blood

21 *TUESDAY*

There was this man
that saved my life
when a man wanted to shoot me down
now I've got problems being grateful

22 *WEDNESDAY*

Men and men and names and names
unexpectedly a woman's name
she's writing a book on men's names

23 *THURSDAY*

Look at some of these men
look at them closely
nothing can shock
their women

24 *FRIDAY*

Sometimes
the gay shirt
is closer to me
than the feminist skirt

25 *SATURDAY*

It's not just the apple:
Eve is also the reason
why Cain flipped out
and Abel never made it

26 *SUNDAY*   Rheumatic couple
seeks ditto
to exchange ideas
et cetera

27 *MONDAY*   There are women I hate
this honorless, defenseless
whimpering female flesh

28 *TUESDAY*   On top of all the bad luck
that befell the great writer
Madame de Sade
divorced him

March

1 *WEDNESDAY*   (Looking into the washing machine):
                     Never again
                     will my socks and shirts
                     form exactly this pattern
                     not in all eternity

2 *THURSDAY*   Under all the car roofs
                     all those deaf cries
                     those stifled grimaces
                     under the glass

3 *FRIDAY*   (The dogs' vengeance):
                     ...that this stinking city
                     right to the last parched lawn
                     is shat brimful
                     full of dogshit

4 *SATURDAY*   Kicking, squalling
                     men in the ball park
                     one, brought down, spreads his legs
                     a reporter scolds shrilly

5 *SUNDAY*   If you look away in embarrassment
                     I'm a cripple
                     if you stare at me reproachfully
                     I'm a fighter

6 *MONDAY*   The winner laughs and the loser weeps
                  no more reason now to weep
                  and no reason yet to laugh
                  fighters grit their teeth

7 *TUESDAY*   I know what I want
                  how I'll reach it
                  what stands in the way
                  how I'll remove the obstacle

8 *WEDNESDAY*   (Woman's Day):
                  An eye for an eye
                  a tooth for a tooth
                  a battering for a battering
                  a rape for a rape

9 *THURSDAY*   (Chapter II of world history):
                  Goddess
                  I thank you
                  that I am not
                  a man

10 *FRIDAY*   What Stalin said about Trotsky
                  Hitler about the jews
                  Freud about women
                  does not interest me

11 *SATURDAY*   *Still and all Sigmund Freud*
                      did some incredible things
                      Still and all Adolf Hitler
                      co-founded Israel

12 *SUNDAY*   (Taking sides):
                      If everyone's for it
                      I am against it
                      if everyone is against it
                      I'm for it

13 *MONDAY*   When the subway train
                      moves more and more slowly
                      and arrives nowhere
                      and the tunnel doesn't stop...

14 *TUESDAY*   You simply throw the keys
                      on the ground
                      that's supposed to mean you're tired
                      and then some

15 *WEDNESDAY*   I write letter after letter
                      to a computer
                      that sends me all my bills
                      in duplicate

16 *THURSDAY*

You toss your head
and purse your lips
what is it you want
to crow or to lay an egg?

17 *FRIDAY*

One more egg
and one more egg
and one more
out of a bloody asshole

18 *SATURDAY*

The clip-clop of horses' hoofs
on our street
everybody throws down their forks
and runs to the window

19 *SUNDAY*

It isn't the weather
it's the family
they're as much fun
as barbed wire

20 *MONDAY*

As though it hadn't
been hurt enough already
my littlest ordinariest toe
is now stomped totally flat

21 *TUESDAY*

You upside down
me right side up
just like a playing card
a bookshelf in the making

22 WEDNESDAY   *(Sailor's true love):*
                     From a ship's rope
                     I knot a doormat for you
                     slowly I begin to understand
                     how the knot got its name

23 THURSDAY   Getting a chinese toy
                     as a present
                     without instructions
                     sharpens your wits

24 FRIDAY   What's the chinese
                     I wonder
                     for what I'd like to
                     say to you?

25 SATURDAY   A life of suffering
                     without the consolations
                     of philosophy and morals
                     and without tears is what I wish for

26 SUNDAY   The ritual easter egg
                     cracked on impact*
                     now I'm afraid
                     for your life again

*Translator's note: At Easter, people take their colored Easter egg and rap
 another person's egg with it. It's bad luck for the one whose egg gets
 cracked.

27 MONDAY

Sooner or later
the silent contest
who'll die
in whose arms

28 TUESDAY

Uncertainty—torture
that I seek to prolong
right until the crash
when certainty breathes a sigh of relief

29 WEDNESDAY

Dear mr. chancellor:
my life has become so short
that I no longer have time
for your problems

30 THURSDAY

A successful work
is like a shipwreck
how do I save myself from the under-
tow
into the smallest boat

31 FRIDAY

To complete a thing
so that it's finished
before it gets broken

April

1 *SATURDAY*

All the beloved things
that get broken
go on ahead of me

2 *SUNDAY*

The leaves die
and are born
and I am born
and die

3 *MONDAY*

So many creatures
haven't lived yet
why should I
take up their space

4 *TUESDAY*

I'm not sitting in the bathtub
and haven't slit open my veins
and yet feel the energy leaving me

5 *WEDNESDAY*

Something that's called *eternal*
drags me behind it
I'm tired to death
I wish the rope would break

THURSDAY

If I'm dead
I have no market value
yet each woman says
Let me die before you

7 FRIDAY

Today I typed all the numerals and characters
on top of one another
a black
death's head appeared

8 SATURDAY

Death solves everything
that weighs on me
so far it hasn't dissolved
the glue called *I*

9 SUNDAY

The heavy, hollow
lump that I am
woke up
and was a kangaroo

10 MONDAY

(mother's lullaby for me):
*Do you know where no
car will run over your tummy?*
in bed.
That's a long time ago

11 TUESDAY	May you get from Schwabing* back to Schwabing unhurt
12 WEDNESDAY	I'm a raving sadist biting your shirt collar naturally you don't scream
13 THURSDAY	Be good to yourself for my sake and that's an order
14 FRIDAY	The great huntresses of Altamira and Lascaux coupling woman with woman they created daughters and images
15 SATURDAY	(1000 x *Women loving women* at the Schwabinger Bräu tavern):* Let's see whether the fact that the women's movement dislikes us will make a full-length feature

---

*Translator's note: Schwabing is the artists' quarter of Munich. The Schwabinger Bräu Tavern is a big beer hall where Franz Josef Strauss gave his pre-election speeches. In 1978, women rented it for a "festival of women loving women" (*Fest der Frauenliebe*). This was a historic event because women could actually publicize it and rent a hall for it—1000 women came.

16 SUNDAY

Nation of free women
lesbian nation
subject to no man
but king alcohol

17 MONDAY

(Woman reporter in the Evening
News):
Men weren't allowed in
I went to the men's room
nobody in there either but lesbians
none of them raped me, though

18 TUESDAY

You've picked a bunch of flowers for
me
Careful you say
There are poisonous weeds among them
So what, that's the way it is

19 WEDNESDAY

The fact that we love each other
in the face of everybody and every-
thing
makes us stronger
than everybody and everything

20 THURSDAY

It's lovely touching
in cotton shirts
lovelier still in silken shirts
loveliest skin to skin

21 *FRIDAY*

Yesterday you
tore up trees by their roots
today I watch over your breath
one leaf after another rights itself

22 *SATURDAY*

You infect the cows
with your
yawn sounding
like cowbells

23 *SUNDAY*

As we eat artichokes
our plates get fuller and fuller
we love each other
more and more every day

24 *MONDAY*

Everything tastes
like biting into paper
if you're not there
to enjoy it with me

25 *TUESDAY*

I close my eyes
and you are there
I open my eyes
and you are there

26 *WEDNESDAY*   (Two old cars at the junkyard):
If we weren't such wrecks
we wouldn't have hit it off with each
other
so well

27 *THURSDAY*   *My angel!*
corny as hell
but true

28 *FRIDAY*   I'm going to exterminate all men
but if *you* were a man
I'd spare you

29 *SATURDAY*   Even if you were a man
I'd love you
So would I
Then we'd be two gay men

30 WALPURGIS
    NIGHT   *(The future's womb conceals*
whether our lot is destined to be dark or
*bright):**
Thanks to male logic, merry widows,
your lot in life is
dark and bright
both at the same time

*Translator's note: Quote from Friedrich Schiller's popular poem, "Das Lied
  von der Glocke."

May

1 MONDAY

Here is a self-created being
not one of my dream images
you are—through and beyond me
your own and separate I

2 TUESDAY

What we have done to each other
is a specter
we cannot kill it
but can forgive it

3 WEDNESDAY

Beneath your face
is a second face
infinitely tender
oh please don't break

4 THURSDAY

Since you began loving me
the dogs no longer bark at me
only a little bird
spattered me with its droppings

5 FRIDAY

I cling
to your solicitude
if I didn't love you
I'd be forever in your debt

6 SATURDAY

You plucked a pitchblack tick
from my backside
once again
you've saved me from a bloodsucker

7 SUNDAY

Shall I despondently
make verses
to a rainy sunday?
Maybe it'll clear up

8 MONDAY

(Remembering May 8, 1945):*
Not one shot had been fired in the city
carts for corpses gathered
the ten thousand dead
women and girls

9 TUESDAY

I focus deep within me
until I feel a stab
I want to help you bear
your pain

10 WEDNESDAY

As I look from the dark into the light
into the shining garden
suddenly she goes
past the window outside

---

*Translator's note: May 8, 1945, was VE (victory in Europe) day. Many women
and girls died as a result of violent acts by the occupying troops.

11 THURSDAY   Watching you
                   work
                   zen and the art
                   of paperhanging

12 FRIDAY   *What is your theory*
                   ideology and moral philosophy?
                   I thought about it and said:
                   The woman I love

13 SATURDAY   The typewriter was
                   what freed me
                   this hammering rage against the boss
                   was really the machine gun

14 SUNDAY   The tree that was planted here
                   at the same time as I was
                   is doing fine
                   how's your tree doing?

15 MONDAY   Jealously
                   I guard this room
                   nobody's allowed to
                   blow smoke at our wallpaper

16 TUESDAY

At first we thought we had the flu
and woke each other up from fainting-
fits
then realized it was
because we were so happy

17 WEDNESDAY

My germs
are your germs
your germs
are my germs

18 THURSDAY

Having hung wallpaper
for two whole weeks
you get down from the ladder
as from a long journey

19 FRIDAY

I am so determinedly your property
that if you did not respect and honor
me
The Story of O would be
horribly true

20 SATURDAY

The bamboo palace
is enormously empty
soon we will have stuffed it
full of problems

21 *SUNDAY*   Depression of the new walls
                                      now I know
                                      that the old crud
                                      was my own

22 *MONDAY*   When preparations for the trip
                                      stop
                                      that IS
                                      the vacation

23 *TUESDAY*   The thunderstorm has passed
                                      the bowling buddies have left
                                      suddenly they're bellowing in the next
                                      room

24 *WEDNESDAY*   The new language: silently
                                      with both hands flat
                                      slapping the steering wheel
                                      several times

25 *THURSDAY*   On this windy, rainy day
                                      two corpuses christi*
                                      decide
                                      to go back to bed

---

*Translator's note: A play on the words *Fronleichnam* (Old High German for
Body of the Lord, a festival celebrated on the Thursday after Trinity Sunday)
and *Leichnam* (modern German for *dead body, corpse*).

26 FRIDAY

A vacation
ruined by rain
means
tears

27 SATURDAY

The roar of the ocean
that stirs the depths of my soul
is only the ventilating system
of the Hotel Sable

28 SUNDAY

Balcony overlooking the ocean
enough sleep
sun and breakfast
fleeting perfection

29 MONDAY

...and next to the bed the refrigerator
which plays with itself
twice an hour
day and night

30 TUESDAY

Round about your sleeping bag
the zipper's crenellations
—fortress walls—
scratch my sunburned skin

31 WEDNESDAY

I'll interpret your dream
of the bellowing men
they actually did bellow
half the night

June

1 THURSDAY

That pygmies shoot small arrows
is no disgrace
that women want to negotiate
is a disgrace

2 FRIDAY

Valerie Solanas started out as a lioness
and ended up in a rathole
it's time we threw out
the baby with the bath water

3 SATURDAY

In this endless feminine rambling
I wish I had encountered
the little word *honor*
one single time

4 SUNDAY

There have been women who had
cancer
and were cured
dishonor is women's only
fatal disease

5 MONDAY

Theologians believe
that I have no soul
I have an honor
and that's enough

6 TUESDAY

As a person of honor and a female
I am not a viable organism
I can do without
the title female

7 WEDNESDAY

Being female is being active-aggressive
it's natural in all living creatures
why, o warped human female
are you afraid of war?

8 THURSDAY

The decline of the west
leaves me cold—but when you drink
beer
while feeding your face with bread and
jam
I could scream

9 FRIDAY

Collect not shells
but fragments of shells on the beach—
with you I want to
form a new pattern

10 SATURDAY

Feeling your head
gently move in my hand
slowly relaxes
my rigidity

11 *SUNDAY*   Our footprints echo
                            in a dark street
                            I close my eyes
                            you carry me

12 *MONDAY*   After two weeks
                            everything is just like home

13 *TUESDAY*   We dreamed the same dream
                            ships wrecked
                            shattered bridge piers
                            and awoke in a thunderstorm

14 *WEDNESDAY*   Now
                            that we're not in public anymore
                            you pig out on garlic

15 *THURSDAY*   Imperturbably
                            I ignore the nightingale
                            and listen:
                            in the bathroom you pull the chain

16 *FRIDAY*

Nothing separates two lovers
more surely
than two sleeping bags
in one car

17 *SATURDAY*

It's raining so hard
we can't camp out
all curses are spent
we're merely "enervated" now

18 *SUNDAY*

If so many adversities
happened to me at home
I'd take my life
every day

19 *MONDAY*

In the car for days
divers inside a bell
down on the ocean floor
in the car we were agreed

20 *TUESDAY*

Just once I'd like to
experience something that can't
possibly
happen to me

21 WEDNESDAY   The longest day
                   on the hill in the park
                   fragrance of jasmine and
                   piles of cigarette butts

22 THURSDAY   Now we resemble the old
                   age-old decrepit couples
                   on etruscan sarcophagus lids
                   who still make love

23 FRIDAY   A word unique to women
                   a loving hmmm
                   that women use to answer women
                   and only women

24 SATURDAY   From time to time
                   we talk
                   of our unhappy love
                   how once you didn't like me

25 SUNDAY   The lawn has grown back
                   that a sadistic scythe
                   mowed
                   from my soul

26 *MONDAY*   Riffling through
                      old pages
                      will bring no
                      new words

27 *TUESDAY*   To break through
                      the ring of superstition
                      not see each other
                      for one day

28 *WEDNESDAY*   Ever since the cat
                      caught the bird
                      she's been a different person

29 *THURSDAY*   In the dream
                      we quarreled and kissed
                      I woke up
                      and we quarreled and kissed

30 *FRIDAY*   Where were you a year ago?
                      Was there a time without you?

July

1 *SATURDAY*   I wish I could
                      shed tears
                      without upsetting you

2 *SUNDAY*   From time to time
                      I feel misunderstood
                      can't say how
                      and ask you to forgive me

3 *MONDAY*   All that you teach me
                      botanical names
                      inexplicable hieroglyphs
                      in my new dreams

4 *TUESDAY*   Carwash
                      Tunnel of horror
                      Holding hands

5 *WEDNESDAY*   It's turned summer
                      we walk through department stores
                      on the same errands
                      as in snow and rain

6 *THURSDAY*   Mentally you follow
                     my itinerary
                     sense it in advance
                     locate its dangers

7 *FRIDAY*   When two non-
                     domesticated animals collide
                     the fur flies
                     even in jest

8 *SATURDAY*   Eating up your memories
                     to incorporate you in myself
                     me as you—
                     I can't manage that

9 *SUNDAY*   Looking down in midkiss
                     at a newspaper page
                     forced to be literate
                     isn't that rape?

10 *MONDAY*   Hand in hand
                     arms swinging
                     playing shopping without money
                     for hours and hours

11 *TUESDAY* The tooth must be filed down
together we go
to a difficult birth

12 *WEDNESDAY* Peace all around us
have we ever
quarreled?

13 *THURSDAY* I visualize
your eyes sewn shut by sleep
but then the clock strikes half past
seven
it's ages since you left the house

14 *FRIDAY* You with your jealousy
are a player
and spoilsport
against one woman who's not playing
the game

15 *SATURDAY* I'm concentrating
on the bump I inflicted on you
whenever it hurts you'll think of me
and I want to feel that I've
comforted you

16 *SUNDAY*

You worry in vain
I didn't take the road
on which your thoughts protect me
at all

17 *MONDAY*

Let black birds fly
thoughts of injustice endured
they keep on returning home

18 *TUESDAY*

On a day
when nothing happens
enough has happened
as it is

19 *WEDNESDAY*

All night
you stood by my bed
—framed—
no wonder you're tired

20 *THURSDAY*

You picked
a thousand blueberries for me
I kiss your thousand
blue fingertips

21 *FRIDAY*   I'd kind of like to
                     just a little bit
                     okay?

22 *SATURDAY*   The fact that perfection
                     won't last
                     hurts me more
                     than failure

23 *SUNDAY*   Reflection
                     moves me to tears
                     thinking straight ahead
                     does not make me cry

24 *MONDAY*   The endless years of torture
                     fly away
                     like one minute of happiness

25 *TUESDAY*   Everything flourishes
                     if I do not exist

26 *WEDNESDAY*   One asshole alone
                     can't be cross-eyed

27 THURSDAY She appeared to us as a monstrosity
and blossomed forth
as a triune sunflower
a holy sight

28 FRIDAY When someone's dead
they've just
gone away
for a moment

29 SATURDAY I take off my glasses
and every thing
leaps in my face

30 SUNDAY A clumsy
couple out on a walk
blocks my view
of you

31 MONDAY M–CN 2879*
that's a poem too

*Translator's note: Munich license plate.

August

1 TUESDAY   Ever since childhood
                     I've been writing the book
                     that doesn't exist
                     that is me

2 WEDNESDAY   Wonder why I
                     no longer see the peak
                     perhaps
                     because I'm practically there

3 THURSDAY   Will you charge me
                     for the detergent too
                     some day?

4 FRIDAY   With open arms
                     you rush
                     toward a sunflower
                     I'm jealous

5 SATURDAY   And for my birthday I'd like
                     a weightlosers' cake
                     every bite I take
                     I'll lose three ounces

6 *SUNDAY*

Some fool, wanting to be the first
calls up and wakes me
birthday morning sun
shines on me and your picture

7 *MONDAY*

Photos—films—television
—misogynist threesome—
how do I watch my step
so "women" don't make it a foursome*

8 *TUESDAY*

Km 0,2—at that milestone
our hearts and backsides
got chilled
a year ago

9 *WEDNESDAY*

Your eyebrows
the outer rim
of creation

10 *THURSDAY*

I arrange
the figures
of your freckles
into a sky full of stars

---

* Translator's note: It is difficult to find a satisfactory English rendition of
this poem: all three media mentioned (*foto—film—fernsehen*) alliterate. The
alliteration would be even more overwhelming if 'woman' (*frau*) were
added to the misogynist (*frauenfeindlich*) threesome.

11 FRIDAY

Wandering over
the landscape of your skin, my eyes
come to rest on monuments
to lost wars

12 SATURDAY

What was most beautiful
about these people
was their countryside
and they ruined it

13 SUNDAY

And that one's found herself a man
and that one hasn't found one
and where's yours
we'll never go home again

14 MONDAY

We decided
you're my *sister-in-law*
but then you got
a heart attack

15 TUESDAY

Introducing you
to a pillar of morality
I have the gall to say
This is my life companion

16 WEDNESDAY   *I'm always hungry*
                  as though someone were eating half my
                  food
                  we both laugh
                  bitterly

17 THURSDAY   I see your sufferings
                  and do not feel them
                  the inside of my mouth turns numb
                  like toothache that has been
                  anesthetized

18 FRIDAY   Sitting on the edge of the bed
                  there is no getting up
                  no lying down
                  no day and night

19 SATURDAY   I dream of Mao and Callas
                  of nothing but the dead
                  and hear your voice in my dream:
                  I don't want to see you any more

20 SUNDAY   Look after yourself
                  carry yourself
                  in front of you
                  like a raw egg

21 MONDAY   Children are born
                     as adults
                     then trained to be
                     children—lifelong children

22 TUESDAY   I am the soldering iron
                     for the pewter coffin
                     you dreamed of

23 WEDNESDAY   Transparent
                     light as a thistledown
                     a gust of wind
                     will carry you away from me

24 THURSDAY   Our bamboo palace
                     is your masterpiece
                     I'm proud
                     it's woman-made

25 FRIDAY   Being so close to you
                     that your two eyes
                     become one single
                     great eye

26 SATURDAY

Drunk as a skunk a maniac
zigzagging toward a child
M—XC 581 Audi 100's
dark orange

27 SUNDAY

Tender living thing
that I hold in my arms
long after
it's gone

28 MONDAY

If you were a sweet little flower
I'd press you
in the phonebook

29 TUESDAY

Now that the lean years are over
we've reached
the era
of snacks

30 WEDNESDAY

At this moment
a woman is sitting somewhere
inventing things
we have a use for

31 THURSDAY

Today I again
stepped aside on the stairs
—automatically—
to avoid a man

September

1 *FRIDAY*   A man can drive
                         as idiotically as he likes
                         his grin proclaims:
                         Here comes an intellectual

2 *SATURDAY*   Judging by the faces of the wives
                         today's an evil day
                         or else the area
                         is misogynist

3 *SUNDAY*   One, being stared at
                         two, hassled and pawed
                         three, always acting
                         as if nothing was happening to you

4 *MONDAY*   Till twenty I was a *thing*
                         till forty a *girl*
                         now I am *grandma*
                         when was I a woman?

5 *TUESDAY*   When you scream at me
                         a tower collapses inside me
                         while you continue to scream
                         I build it again

6 *WEDNESDAY*   None of the rugs are
                 the way we wanted them
                 so we bought ourselves
                 a loom

7 *THURSDAY*   My lover inspects
                 my collected works
                 Our poems are more beautiful
                 she says

8 *FRIDAY*   Once you told me not to
                 say *mine* to you
                 now we can't keep the *me-you*
                 apart any more

9 *SATURDAY*   There must never
                 be a sign here
                 saying, *This was*
                 a forest

10 *SUNDAY*   A leaf, released
                 snows down on graves
                 uncramping
                 coronary vessel spasms

11 MONDAY　　　　We stir
　　　　　　　　　　the dregs
　　　　　　　　　　of our coffee
　　　　　　　　　　and drink the sugar

12 TUESDAY　　　　Death is painless
　　　　　　　　　　what hurts
　　　　　　　　　　is still being alive

13 WEDNESDAY　　*I'm glad*
　　　　　　　　　　to be alive
　　　　　　　　　　bitter
　　　　　　　　　　words

14 THURSDAY　　　Every day
　　　　　　　　　　drops from the sky
　　　　　　　　　　and the earth
　　　　　　　　　　covers it up

15 FRIDAY　　　　I do not see
　　　　　　　　　　the wind and time
　　　　　　　　　　how do I know
　　　　　　　　　　that they come and go

16 *SATURDAY*   Intertwined for
four hundred years
like the two ash trees
in the Dachau Moor

17 *SUNDAY*   I place two cups
on the breakfast table
then remember
I am alone

18 *MONDAY*   There's one christa reinig
you say—that I don't know
that's the poet.
—I don't know her either—

19 *TUESDAY*   A time when I existed
and your eyes, your hands
did not?
that can't have been so

20 *WEDNESDAY*   Even in dreams I am not alone
helpful, you go with me
giving advice—sometimes
scolding

21 THURSDAY   We gaze at each other
                      endlessly at each other
                      the TV show goes on
                      without us

22 FRIDAY   Milfoil* shared with another
                      is five-hundred-
                      foil
                      still bitter enough

23 SATURDAY   If only we'd always keep on
                      walking like this
                      straight ahead...

24 SUNDAY   Pouring coffee
                      without hindrance
                      happy
                      afternoon

25 MONDAY   Looking out the window
                      at the road
                      you're walking through branches
                      as though through green air

---

*Translator's note: "milfoil" is not an exact translation; the problem here is translating a double pun—"Geteilte Freude ist doppelte Freude," "Joy shared is joy doubled"; and a pun on two people sharing an herbal tea called *Tausendgüldenkraut*, centaury ("one thousand guilder weed"), and thus getting "500 guilders" apiece. Milfoil ("1000 leaves"), aka yarrow, comes closest to this pun. It is also an herbal tea, and very bitter.

26 TUESDAY

If you think of me
I flourish
from afar
you make my path smooth

27 WEDNESDAY

We are the new human being
and this new human being
is not a man

28 THURSDAY

You dream: I am killing myself
wake up with a scream
and are angry at me

29 FRIDAY

(Threefold cause
for bliss):
that you exist
that I exist
that we exist

30 SATURDAY

People live
without us
and here we are
racking our brains

October

1 *SUNDAY*   When I am sad
                     I have to
                     put myself down on the earth
                     like a rock

2 *MONDAY*   I crawled over a plowed field
                     and it destroyed me
                     I came into a forest
                     and it raised me up

3 *TUESDAY*   It's half-past six
                     I'm waiting for you
                     whether you come or not
                     I'll wait

4 *WEDNESDAY*   I don't want
                     to be reborn
                     in better universes
                     but here with you

5 *THURSDAY*   My great flights of fancy
                     are gone
                     I am coarse-grained
                     gravity-drawn

6 FRIDAY

A boy that pees on
his little sister
should have his head
dashed against the wall

7 SATURDAY

Get raped
if that doesn't
destroy you
you were already destroyed

8 SUNDAY

The man
is the head
once the head's gone
the man's gone

9 MONDAY

Doctors are a sickness
it sickens me
that I need them

10 TUESDAY

Afternoon at the academy
evening at the women's center
Dr. Jekyll
and Sister Gin

11 WEDNESDAY   (Herb tea):
                     The important thing is
                     that we have it together
                     not whether we
                     have champagne

12 THURSDAY   Why did I run to
                     the window?
                     I don't know
                     then I see your car

13 FRIDAY   Catching a bird—comedy
                     for one character
                     the cat laughs
                     enough for two

14 SATURDAY   This may be
                     the last fine day
                     we don't mind giving it up
                     there are too many enjoying it

15 SUNDAY   At last we've learned
                     to fight about money
                     that's firm ground
                     under our feet

16 *MONDAY*

I'm not what I
had in mind
but I've
accepted myself

17 *TUESDAY*

I'm your seeing-eye dog
you say
you're my eyesight
I say

18 *WEDNESDAY*

I wish I had a nightshirt
with blue-and-white diamonds*
Ha! you shout, *No way,
not for a prussian!*

19 *THURSDAY*

Having money
and not having any
are two non-interchangeable
states of consciousness

20 *FRIDAY*

I shall
always love you
with and without
your pimples

*Translator's note: White and blue: the colors of the Bavarian royal house.

21 *SATURDAY*   A goldfinch looks
                     tremendously self-assured
                     there's no such thing as
                     an anxious bird face

22 *SUNDAY*   *Look, a crested lark!*
                     maybe it's a canary
                     whose hair
                     is standing on end

23 *MONDAY*   You sure are good at cursing
                     you can curse
                     the head
                     off a glass of pale ale

24 *TUESDAY*   We pretend we're doing karate
                     Asshole!
                     you yell
                     (I'm always with you)

25 *WEDNESDAY*   Was this the first
                     or the last time
                     we climbed
                     the Brauneck?

26 *THURSDAY*

Besides all the things that I owe you
here is one more: being able to climb
mountains with honest-to-goodness
mountain boots

27 *FRIDAY*

I talk to your picture
it offers
no resistance

28 *SATURDAY*

Your hands cool
my sweatdrenched hair
in my hair
you warm your frozen hands

29 *SUNDAY*

We're a double-edged
saw on people's
nerves—'cause
we're doing fine

30 *MONDAY*

From a dark gateway
I step out
into the sunlight
that's how I want to die

31 *TUESDAY*

With leaden feet
I follow a shadow
I call its name
and awake with my name

November

1 WEDNESDAY   Life is senseless
                     if I forget that
                     I am blind
                     if I think of it—lame

2 THURSDAY   In the house
                     of trust
                     there are no
                     keys

3 FRIDAY   A real heart
                     can't ever
                     break
                     often enough

4 SATURDAY   Sheep do not gather
                     around the butcher
                     the shepherd
                     does not smell of blood

5 SUNDAY   My hands encircle
                     your presence
                     I cannot grasp
                     all you are to me

6 MONDAY
Latest report
the world will not come to an end
but it isn't saved
either

7 TUESDAY
(*Triumph of the Will*):
There's a state of being trampled
that leaves you no other choice
than to be nice to each other

8 WEDNESDAY
When I was going to be shot
my mother repudiated me
today I know the reason
she had to survive me

9 THURSDAY
I've sunk so low
that your linen sleeve
is a holier sight for me
than all these godlike gurus

10 FRIDAY
Our happiness is a nest egg
we brood over it
with the tenderest down

11 SATURDAY   How often
                     at night in dreams
                     we have managed
                     without each other

12 SUNDAY   The broken tea ball
                     from our vacation
                     thrown out at last
                     it wrenches me again

13 MONDAY   Some nameless
                     calamity
                     must simply be
                     obliterated by silence

14 TUESDAY   *Death—a new beginning*
                     without you?
                     I do not want this beginning

15 WEDNESDAY   We no longer argue
                     we throw dice
                     whichever of us throws a six
                     must keep her trap shut

16 *THURSDAY*   What did you dream
when I dreamed
you were in danger?

17 *FRIDAY*   You read aloud to me
I spell out
your fingers, your nails
the half-moons on your fingernails

18 *SATURDAY*   The sauerkraut
is on the table
we assure each other
we're doing fine

19 *SUNDAY*   I get three wishes:
that you finally give me a haircut
and secondly and thirdly
not too long and not too short

20 *MONDAY*   Oh for a stream of Pompeiian lava
to flow over us
keep us motionless
till the end of the earth

21 TUESDAY
Iranian women
wrapped in black coffins
from head to foot
beat me to death

22 WEDNESDAY
Unexpectedly encountering
a dead body
I am plunged back
into my beginning

23 THURSDAY
Who is the sparrow-hawk
you dreamed of?
Who is the dove
I dreamed of?

24 FRIDAY
Nothing harder
than showing
an ass
its own hole

25 SATURDAY
You dream I am a bird
you dream I am a river
you dream I am a ring on your hand
with a stone that weighs a ton

26 *MEMORIAL DAY FOR THE DEAD*
And maybe our next car
will be a mercedes
black
with one of those silver palm trees

27 *MONDAY*
I lay my forehead
on your forehead
for one endless
moment

28 *TUESDAY*
Your family wants first
that I shouldn't exist—second
that I should save you—third
that I should be to blame for your
death

29 *WEDNESDAY*
Women are rivers
that have never
reached the sea
not up to now

30 *THURSDAY*
The yarn on your knitting
somehow it manages
to keep things going

December

1 *FRIDAY*   Ripped apart
                     day after day
                     sewn together
                     day after day

2 *SATURDAY*   The cruel things that are done to me
                     the cruel things that are done to you
                     collect in bags
                     that we throw at each other's heads

3 *SUNDAY*   Midnight and the first snowfall
                     you scratch away on your car
                     for a whole fifteen minutes
                     while I listen as though through cotton
                     wool

4 *MONDAY*   Christmas shoppers
                     by a war memorial
                     bombed, shattered
                     snowed in

5 *TUESDAY*   Now you climb
                     the plum tree
                     I wait for what
                     will be left over for me

6 WEDNESDAY   According to the chinese horoscope
                we'll never meet
                how lucky
                we're not in China

7 THURSDAY   Promise me
                that you're happy
                that's basically
                it

8 FRIDAY   I place my hands
                on mirror glass
                that way they lie on the icy road
                you cross it safely

9 SATURDAY   *I'm not gonna*
                sell myself!
                I don't have to buy you
                you are a gift

10 SUNDAY   All the tenderness
                of monkeys—when I
                scratch your back

11 MONDAY   I ask your picture
                      where are you?
                      are you all right?
                      no answer

12 TUESDAY   I wish it were night
                      all the guests would have left the house
                      and the two of us
                      would be left alone

13 WEDNESDAY   Behind the neighbor's wall
                      is Auschwitz
                      keep your trap shut
                      or it'll be your turn

14 THURSDAY   As for the human race, you say
                      you feel no compassion for it
                      and I, you say, am also
                      only human

15 FRIDAY   *Hey scratch my back*
                      up there—higher
                      now toward the window
                      now toward the wall

16 *SATURDAY*   A woman has woven fabric for the suit
a woman has set up the mikes
a woman has typed documents
his excellency gives an interview

17 *SUNDAY*   Falling
through
a pile of shit
into a goldmine

18 *MONDAY*   If instead of you I had
Saint Augustine
what would I do with him?

19 *TUESDAY*   You're doing fine
you say
your nostrils
gaze at me sadly

20 *WEDNESDAY*   At that point you didn't exist
at this point your heart had begun to
beat
then your breathing set in
then you came into being for me

21 THURSDAY   People like us
                      have guardian angels
                      that work overtime

22 FRIDAY   Had a bad dream?
                      Not even in your dream
                      can I leave you
                      defenseless

23 SATURDAY   When we're doing well
                      our pendulums swing
                      yours to the right—mine to the left
                      we have the loveliest fights

24 SUNDAY   Never before
                      have I had
                      my hair cut with nail scissors
                      on christmas eve

25 MONDAY   Merry Christmas
                      from nightgown
                      to nightgown

26 TUESDAY

Out of us will arise
beings
that will not be born
on this earth

27 WEDNESDAY

A life is like a ring
that we draw
on each other's finger
every day

28 THURSDAY

What's left
of me—loves
what's left
of you

29 FRIDAY

There'll be a box put in front of the door
a sign saying: *Please*
throw in money
and leave us alone

30 SATURDAY

Would you have thought
we'd make it
this far?

31 SUNDAY

We turned over
and were a year older

SOME NOTES ABOUT THE TRANSLATION

In her texts, Christa Reinig consistently goes against the grain of German spelling by using capitals only for proper nouns, beginnings of sentences, and nouns in quotes from other authors, while she uses lower case for all other German nouns (which are normally capitalized). To preserve the flavor of her lack of orthodoxy, only proper nouns and titles were capitalized in this translation, while adjectives and nouns like "chinese," "black," and "jew" were left in lower case.

I'm also trying to make Reinig's language more inclusive. The German "einer" (one) is masculine and so all agreements should be masculine (July 18). However, in *recent* years German feminists have been using "eine" and feminine agreements ("she"). The colloquial "someone"/"they" fits in with the overall colloquial tone of Reinig's language, and is more inclusive (Cf. "everybody throws down their forks"—March 18).

Ilze Mueller
Translator

CHRISTA REINIG

Christa Reinig was born in Berlin in 1926, attended school there, and was a florist's apprentice. She later did clerical work, then worked in factories and in construction. From 1953 until 1957 she studied art history and Christian archeology at the Humbolt University. Until 1963, she was a scientific assistant at the Märkisches Museum in East Berlin. In 1964 she was given the Bremen Prize for Literature and has since been living in the Federal German Republic. She is a member of PEN, of the Munich Tukankreis, and of the Bavarian Academy of Fine Arts. In 1965/66, she was awarded the Villa Massimo fellowship, in 1968 the Prize for Radio Plays of the veterans blinded in the war, in 1969 the Tukan Prize of the City of Munich, and in 1976 the German Critics' Prize for Literature.

Her publications include: *Die Steine von Finisterre*, poems (1960); *Der Traum meiner Verkommenheit* (1961); *Gedichte*, poems (1963); *Drei Schiffe* (1965); *Schwabinger Marterln* (1969); *Orion trat aus dem Haus* (1969); *Schwalbe von Olevano*, poems (1969); *Das grosse Bechterew-Tantra* (1970); *Papantscha Vielerlei* (1971); *Hantipanti* (1972); *Die Ballade vom blutigen Bomme* (1972); *Die himmlische und die irdische Geometrie*, novel (1975); *Der Hund mit dem Schlussel* (1976); *Entmannung*, novel (1976); *Drei Schiffe* (1978); *Mußiggang ist aller Liebe Anfang*, poems (1979); *Die Prufung des Lachlers*, poems (1980); *Der Wolf und die Witwen*, stories and essays (1979); *Die ewige Schule*, stories (1982); *Die Frau im Brunnen*, novel (1984); *Nobody*, short stories (1989); *Glück und Glas*, short stories (1991); and *Ein Wogenzug von wilden Schwänen*, poems (1991).

She has also written numerous radio plays, a translation of the poems of Marina Tsvetaeva, and has been published in *Die schwarze Botin, Frauenoffensive Journal,* and *Münchner Frauenzeitung.*

ILZE MUELLER

Born in Cesis, Latvia, Ilze Mueller lived in Germany and Australia before moving to the United States, where she makes her permanent home. She has also lived in Tanzania and Zaire. A graduate of the University of Chicago and University of Minnesota, with master's and doctoral degrees in German literature, she is a member of the Department of German and Russian Studies at Macalester College in St. Paul, Minnesota. She has taught German at several other Twin Cities colleges and universities.

A recipient of a Fulbright Fellowship and the Canadian *Jauna Gaita* Translation Prize, Ms. Mueller has been translating German and Latvian poetry and prose into English since the 1970's. Her translations have appeared in *Conditions* and *Nimrod*. Recently she has begun writing poetry and is published in *Looking for Home* (Milkweed, 1990). *Idleness Is the Root of All Love* is her first book-length translation.

ANGELIKA BAMMER

An assistant professor of German and Women's Studies at Emory University, Angelika Bammer has written widely on contemporary women's literature, German culture, feminist theory and women's movement politics. Her forthcoming book is *Partial Visions: Feminism and Utopianism in the 1970's* (London: Routledge, 1991). Born in West Germany, Ms. Bammer resides in Atlanta, Georgia.

Colophon

The text for this book was composed in Palatino.
Typeset by ImPrint Services, Corvallis, Oregon.